2

MW01715533

ERIE CANAL

ERIE CANAL
GATEWAY TO THE WEST

BY NICHOLAS NIRGIOTIS

A FIRST BOOK

New York / Chicago / London / Sydney

Franklin Watts

J386.48
N629e

3 1466 00309 7769

MAIN LIBRARY
WARREN TRUMBULL CO. PUBLIC LIBRARY

10-15-93

Photographs copyright ©: University of Rochester Library, 2–3; North Wind Picture Archives, 9, 10, 13 (top & bottom), 15 (top & bottom), 32, 39, 44, 46; The New-York Historical Society, 17, 25, 43; Canal Museum, Syracuse, NY, 23, 28, 30, 40, 57; New York Public Library, 31; De Witt Clinton High School, Courtesy Margaret Yardley Voelker, 36; New York State Historical Association, 49; The Portrait Place, 52; International Museum of Photography at George Eastman House, 54 (top & bottom).

Library of Congress Cataloging-in-Publication Data

Nirgiotis, Nicholas.
Erie Canal : gateway to the West / by Nicholas Nirgiotis.
p. cm. — (A First book)
Includes bibliographical references and index.
Summary: Describes the building of the Erie Canal and discusses its historical, political, economic, and sociological impact on the country.
ISBN 0-531-20146-5 (HC, library binding)
1. Erie Canal (N.Y.—History—Juvenile literature. [1. Erie Canal (N.Y.)—History.] I. Title.
II. Series.
HE396.E6N77 1993
386'.48'09747—dc20 92-24547 CIP AC

Copyright © 1993 by Nicholas Nirgiotis
All rights reserved
Printed in the United States of America
6 5 4 3 2 1

CONTENTS

CHAPTER ONE

A NATION DIVIDED

JUST AFTER THE UNITED STATES became independent, the frontiersmen and the hunters who ventured westward from the Atlantic seacoast sent back home wonderful stories. They told of a land teeming with deer, beaver, bear, and buffalo and so fertile that corn grew as high as a barn. A man could ride for days, they said, through flat, green meadows that stretched from the Ohio to the Mississippi rivers and north to the Great Lakes.

For many thousands of men and women who lived in crowded cities in the East or in rural areas where there was not enough good farmland to go around, the lure of the lush western lands was hard to resist. They had dreamed of a farm of their own that would yield rich crops; it now seemed possible to have it. All they had to do to claim their share of the promised land was cross over the Appalachian Mountains.

The trouble was that the way west was difficult. The Appalachians rose like a wall from New England to the Deep South, barring the way to all but the most daring.

The few who headed west on horseback discovered it took a stout heart and cool nerves to ride the rough Indian foot trails that snaked their way through the shadowy woods and over the mountain passes. Passengers in wagons or stagecoaches had an even more miserable time. They swayed, lurched, and bounced every foot of the way on muddy, rutted roads that wore out both horses and axles and left a lasting impression on all who traveled them.

A spiteful nature, it seemed, had set up the Appalachians to divide the nation in two and keep emigration west to a trickle. What the new American nation needed urgently was an easy road through the mountains to bring people to the new lands and promote trade between East and West.

The Appalachian Mountains *formed a rugged barrier that made westward travel torturous.*

DEEP WOODED VALLEYS *and steeply rising hills challenged travelers crossing the mountains. Trails were just wide enough for a pack horse.*

There were political reasons as well for bringing the two parts of the youthful United States together without delay. General George Washington, who in 1784 had traveled westward through upper New York State to the shores of Lake Erie, understood as well as anyone that unless the West was bound to the Atlantic states through trade, it might eventually go its separate way and set itself up as an independent nation.

Early travelers in the West had learned from the Indians that lakes and rivers were the best highways, and that it was easier to paddle a canoe or pole a raft than to walk. Not only was this the fastest, most comfortable way to travel, but it was also the cheapest way to transport goods.

If this was the best way to go, then, possibly, the solution for a route through the mountains lay in upstate New York. The key was the Mohawk River, which had carved a natural path through the Appalachians to the Hudson River. The Mohawk Valley offered the only break in the entire wall of mountains from north to south.

There were problems, however. The Mohawk was full of obstructions that were dangerous to navigation. There were rapids, waterfalls, and shallows along its course, and in the summer the river ran dry in places. The solution that had seemed so close remained as far away as ever.

CHAPTER TWO

FROM VISION INTO LAW

RIVERS ARE UNGOVERNABLE things," Benjamin Franklin had said. But a canal running parallel to the Mohawk River through the Appalachians would be an entirely different matter. Once it was past the mountains, the canal would span the wilderness of upper New York to link the Hudson River with Lake Erie and the interior. Its waters would flow smoothly and safely to open the continent to settlement and trade.

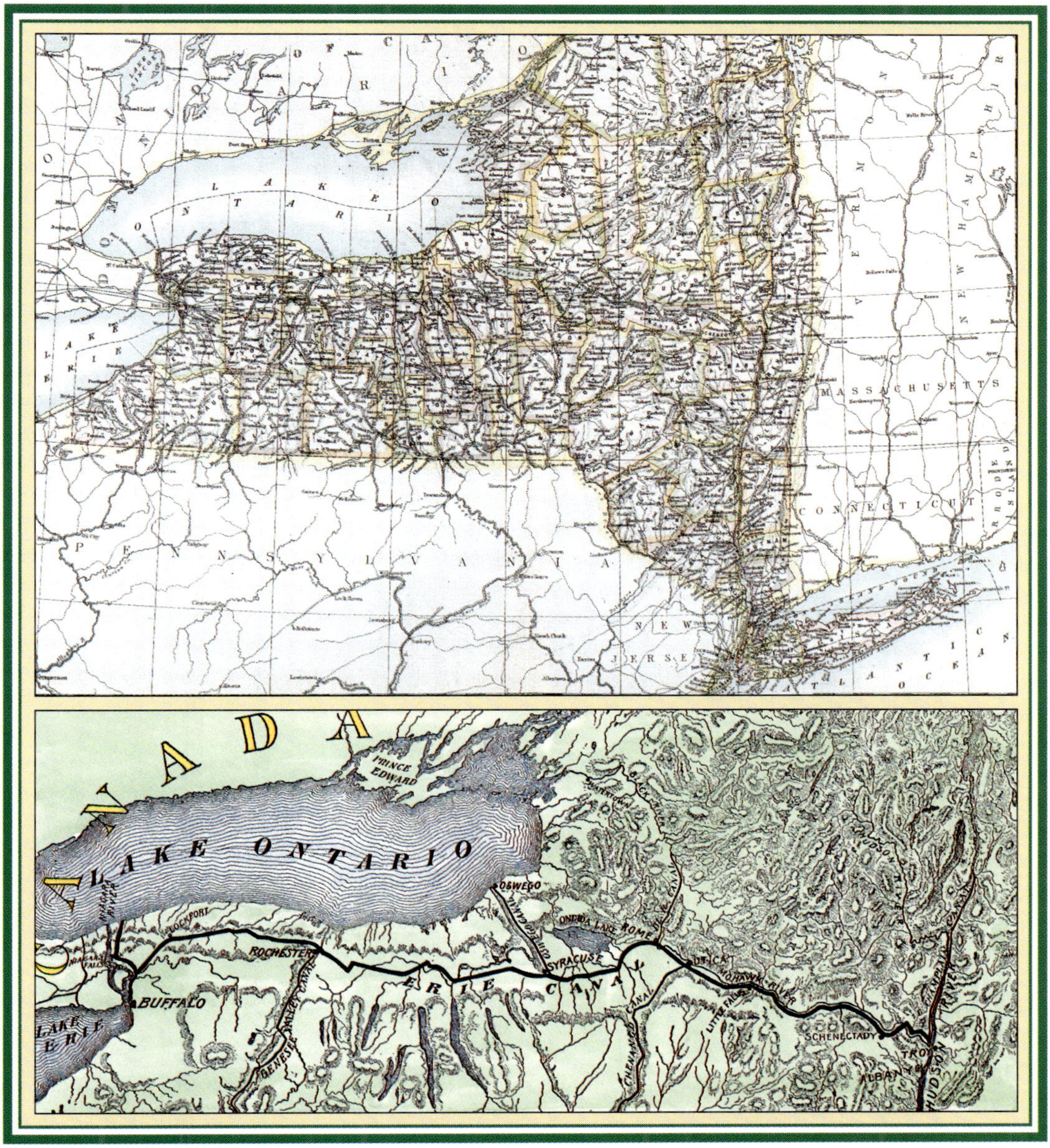

Top, map of New York *state. Bottom, the Erie Canal ran across upper New York from the Hudson River to Buffalo.*

Although others had suggested the idea before, the first person to propose a well-thought-out plan for a canal across upper New York State was Jesse Hawley. He was a flour merchant in Geneva, New York, who was familiar with the difficulty and expense of shipping goods to and from the west.

In 1807, Hawley published a local newspaper article that caught the imagination of his readers. Soon popular pressure forced the New York State legislature to authorize a survey to seek the best possible route for the canal.

James Geddes, the surveyor appointed to the job, was a lawyer and businessman with some experience in surveying. This was not an unusual situation. Practically none of the people who eventually worked on the canal had any experience in building canals. Yet this did not prove to be a handicap. Ingenuity filled the gaps in their knowledge or experience. Later, Geddes was to become one of the chief engineers on the Erie, along with Benjamin Wright.

Geddes looked at three proposed routes. One, the shortest, would connect the Hudson River with Lake Ontario. The second was a route between Lakes Erie and Ontario and around Niagara Falls. The third would run from the Hudson westward across a 363-mile (580-km) wilderness to Lake Erie. Geddes recommended the third route, even though

JAMES GEDDES, *top, and Benjamin Wright, bottom, were selected to serve as chief engineers for the Erie Canal.*

it was the longest and costliest, because the route to Lake Ontario would have benefited Canada more than the United States.

The next step was to find the estimated $6 million that this enormous project would cost. Because this was a huge sum in those days for just one state to spend, the planners decided to appeal to the federal government in Washington, D.C., for financial help.

In 1809, a two-man delegation took the surveyor's recommendations to President Thomas Jefferson and made a strong case for the canal. This appeal was to no avail. The project was a splendid one, the president agreed, but it was too difficult and too costly for the resources of the new country.

Instead of discouraging the canal planners, however, Jefferson's rejection strengthened their will to go ahead. And it gave them a brilliant idea. They decided that what they needed more than money at this stage was a man with the skills and influence to convince New York State lawmakers to approve the project.

The man they chose to lead the fight for the Erie Canal was the mayor of New York City, De Witt Clinton. Clinton had previously served in the U.S. Senate, and he was the leader of his party in the state. He was a strongminded person and a popu-

De Witt Clinton, *a leading New York political figure, was the moving force behind the building of the Erie.*

lar politician. From the moment he agreed to support construction of the Erie Canal, no one devoted more time and energy to its success than he did. There is little doubt that without Clinton's help, the Erie Canal would not have been built.

His task was not an easy one. The Erie Canal faced strong opposition from both politicians and businessmen in New York City who feared competition from the west. Many other people thought the taxes they would have to pay for its construction would primarily benefit the area served by the canal. Because Clinton had been a dynamic mayor of the city and had a large personal following there, supporters figured he could be counted on to overcome this opposition.

They were right. Clinton was able to organize support for the project, and in 1810 the state legislature created the Erie Canal Commission. During the summer of 1810, the commission made a month-long survey of the canal route to get firsthand knowledge of the problems the builders would have to face. It recommended unanimously that the canal should be built and financed directly by the state.

The War of 1812–15 against Great Britain brought planning to a halt. But as soon as the fighting was over, there was an immediate push for action. A petition was circulated pointing out the benefits of the canal and the riches it would bring to the state, and more than one hundred thousand signatures were collected. The war helped, too. It showed how difficult it was to move men and supplies to fight the enemy without a good transportation system.

In the spring of 1817, Clinton was elected governor of New York by a vote of 43,000 to 1,500. It was a triumph for Clinton, and for the canal as well. From his position as governor, Clinton continued to speak and write about the benefits to be gained from the canal. "One day when the canal is finished, New York City will stand unrivaled by any city on the face of the earth," he proclaimed to his fellow citizens.

Despite the powerful opposition, pressure for the canal was building all the time. There were merchants who wanted to sell their goods in the West, farmers who wanted to migrate to the new lands, and many other people who stood to benefit in various ways from this grand project.

Clinton's voice and the demands of the people who wanted the canal to be built increased the pressure on the lawmakers. Finally, in April 1817, after many years of dreaming and planning, construction of the Erie Canal was approved by the New York legislature.

CHAPTER THREE

DIGGING THE "GRAND CANAL"

THE POLITICIANS HAD ACTED. Now it was up to the builders to dig their ditch through the rough terrain, the forests, and the swamps over which the canal had to be built. All this had to be done without the help of trained civil engineers to mastermind the work, for no one knew much about canal building in the United States at that time. In fact, the canal itself became effectively the first school of civil engineering.

To keep costs to a minimum, the commission decided the channel should be 40 feet (13 m) wide and just 4 feet (1.2 m) deep. From end to end, the Erie would be 363 miles (580 km) long. All along the canal there would be a 10-foot (3-m) wide tow-path on one side for the horses and mules to walk as they pulled, or towed, the canal boats, which had no engines or sails.

Because Lake Erie is 565 feet (170 m) higher than the Hudson River, eighty-three locks would be needed to step the boats up or down, depending on the direction they were traveling. In places, aqueducts would have to be built to carry the canal over deep valleys or streams.

Work began July 4, 1817, in Rome, New York. The canal commissioners had decided to begin digging the middle section of the canal first because the ground there was level and soft, and they could make faster progress. Bulldozers and steam shovels were unknown in those days, so workers had to dig, scrape, and haul the earth with the primitive tools available to them. Axmen cleared the brush and the trees. Fallen trees were dragged away, and then the pick and shovel work began. As the mounds of earth were carted away by wheelbarrow, supervisors measured the depth of the trench.

Removing the trees covering the path that the canal followed was backbreaking, time-consuming work. Many thousands of oaks, elms, and hickories had to be cut down by hand. It was soon obvious that unless an easier way were found, the work would not progress quickly.

Before long, a machine was improvised to do the job. Workers tied a chain to the top of each tree and ran the other end to a large wheel turned by a screw gear. When the gear was turned by a crank, it produced a force strong enough to topple the tree to the ground. A mechanical "stump puller" was also devised to remove stubborn tree stumps from the ground.

After all the trees and brush had been removed, workers leveled small hills, filled in low spots, and built embankments to hold the sides together. Only then could workers come along to begin digging the narrow, shallow ditch.

Special cement capable of hardening underwater was needed to hold the stone used in building the locks and to make the aqueducts waterproof. Importing the cement from Europe would have been too expensive. Canvass White, an assistant engineer, discovered a kind of limestone near the canal that made an excellent waterproof cement when ground to powder form and mixed with sand. This saved the canal project.

At first, local farmers and their helpers were hired to dig sections of the canal. But at the end of

NEAR LOCKPORT WORKMEN *had to cut and blast a channel through solid rock. Large cranes were used to lift out the rubble.*

the first season, they were replaced by regular laborers and recently arrived immigrants. It seemed logical that a permanent work force would do the job faster and better.

By the summer of 1819, the canal had reached the Montezuma swampland, a desolate area west of Syracuse. This land was thick with tall reeds and filled with stagnant water. Laborers had to dig while standing in water up to their knees, only to see the soil from the sides ooze back into the ditch. But discomfort and frustration were not their only problems.

The swamp was home to hordes of mosquitoes that swarmed over the crews in great clouds, day and night, biting every exposed part of their bodies and making sleep impossible. And every bite carried with it the risk of death, for the mosquitoes spread disease. Hundreds of men came down with chills and fever. Many died; others fled to save their lives.

But other workers endured the hardships and the sickness, and the work continued. The dead were buried, and slowly, very slowly, the living made their way through the swamp. Cold weather helped end the misery. An early frost killed the mosquitoes and hardened the soil. Workers could now dig without fear that the banks would ooze away.

Success in the swamp not only raised the confidence of the builders, it also boosted the chances the state would approve the construction of the other two sections of the waterway. To make sure of continued support, in 1819 the commissioners decided to open to boat traffic the small section of the Erie Canal already completed from Utica to Rome.

A PAINTING BY *John William Hill shows workmen shoring up the towpath as the canal boat Rochester moves past.*

This would be the first real test of the canal because no one yet knew whether the walls would withstand the pressure of the water and remain firm. Sluice gates were opened, and water from nearby feeder streams and rivers began to trickle in and then flow faster into the channel. As the water crept upward, there was great anxiety all along the line. But the engineers and the crews had done their work well. Everything held as planned.

Soon boats were floating in the canal, and everyone could now see that real progress had been made. The following year, the first passenger boats made their way from Rome to Syracuse.

Even though it was only partially completed, the canal was in business, and large amounts of money were being collected from tolls. The builders were pleased with the success they had achieved so far, but they had reason to worry because trouble lurked ahead. The next two sections of the canal waiting to be built would present new engineering problems that might prove to be unbeatable.

CHAPTER FOUR

TO ALBANY AND BUFFALO

GOING EASTWARD FROM ROME to Albany, where the canal would connect with the Hudson River, the land dropped more than 400 feet (121 m) in height. To help boats step up or down this incline, builders constructed fifty-three locks, as they were needed along the way.

A canal cannot slope too sharply because its water would then rush downward, making navigation impossible. So when a boat going toward Albany had to drop to a lower level because of the natural slope, it entered a shoe-box-like lock

A CANAL BOAT LEAVES THE LOCK *at Delta Dam. A lock raises or lowers a boat by controlling the level of the water.*

through large gates. After the gates closed tightly, the water in the chamber of the lock was drained away slowly through a small hatch at the bottom of the exit gate until it was level with the water on the lower level. The exit gate at the opposite end of the lock was then opened, and the boat was free to continue its trip. Going toward Buffalo, boats were raised to a higher level at each lock by reversing the procedure.

To pass through the narrow Mohawk Valley, the canal had to cross over the Mohawk River twice. The only way to do this each time was to put the canal on aqueducts, water-carrying bridges supported on stone arches.

Westward toward Lake Erie, the canal was built along a ridge on the edge of the Irondequoit Valley. The channel was cut into the side of the ridge and the towpath followed a manmade embankment. From the valley below, the canal resembled a skyway. The Erie crossed the rough Genesee River near Rochester on an 800-foot (242-m) aqueduct built on top of nine stone arches. This was the longest stone arch bridge in the world at that time. Boats floated high over the racing waters of the river to the wonder of passengers and spectators.

Early in 1824, a group of De Witt Clinton's political enemies succeeded in having him dismissed

A WATER-CARRYING BRIDGE, *called an aqueduct, helped boats cross the Mohawk River at Little Falls.*

The aqueduct at Rochester *was famed as the longest stone bridge of its day. It spanned the Genessee River on nine graceful arches.*

from the Erie Canal Commission. With this desperate move, they hoped to scuttle the project and deny Clinton any recognition for what he had accomplished. But Clinton would not be out of office long. Citizens voiced their outrage at his ouster in mass protests. To them, Clinton was the Erie Canal and the Erie Canal was Clinton. Growing toll collec-

AT LOCKPORT THE ERIE *climbed up the steeply rising face of a cliff on a double set of five locks, one set for eastbound traffic, the other for westbound.*

tions in the sections already operating also helped change people's minds about the canal. In November 1824, Clinton was elected governor once again by a landslide.

Getting the canal up a steep rock face at Lockport, northeast of Buffalo, was the last major construction challenge. To conquer this rock wall, engineer Nathan Roberts designed five locks for eastbound traffic and five for westbound. The Lockport Five, as they came to be known, were cut out of solid rock in successive steps. With the help of this "staircase," boats could climb up and down the 60-foot (18-m) wall gently and safely in five giant steps.

Once on top of the cliff, it was necessary to cut deeply through solid rock. Because it was impossible to break the hard rock with picks and shovels, digging was done by stuffing blasting powder in holes drilled into the rock and then exploding the charge.

The Lockport section was the most difficult and the most expensive part of the canal. Despite the difficulties, work progressed on schedule. Crews were eager to meet the deadline, set for the end of summer, so the canal could be opened in October 1825, as promised by Clinton.

CHAPTER FIVE

THE WEDDING OF THE WATERS

THE WEATHER REMAINED MILD throughout the summer and early fall, and on the date set in October, the full length of the Erie Canal, from Albany to Buffalo, was ready to be opened to traffic. The dream had finally become a reality.

On October 26, 1825, the canal boat *Seneca Chief* with De Witt Clinton, Jesse Hawley, and other dignitaries aboard, started its historic voyage from Buffalo toward New York City. To announce the news that the canal was officially open, a primitive telegraph was devised. Cannon set within hearing distance of each other were fired down the line all the way from Buffalo to New York City. Within eighty-one minutes, New Yorkers had heard the news.

At every town along the route, there were brass bands, banquets, and speeches praising Clinton and the builders of the canal. Cannon fired salutes, and there were toasts and ribbon-cutting ceremonies. As it made its triumphant way eastward, the *Seneca Chief* was followed by a small fleet of other canal boats.

From Albany, the flotilla was towed by steamboats down the Hudson to New York City, where it arrived on November 4. The attitude of New Yorkers toward Clinton and the canal had begun to change even while the Erie was partially in operation. People were now grateful because the canal was bringing the wealth of interior America to their port. Clinton was the hero of the hour, and he received a hero's welcome.

A multitude of ships of all sizes and from many nations accompanied the *Seneca Chief* as it moved to Sandy Hook at the entrance of the harbor climaxing the celebration in a formal ceremony called the "Wedding of the Waters." Governor Clinton poured Lake Erie water he had carried in casks from

"The Wedding of the Waters" *celebration in New York City marked the opening of the canal. Clinton poured water from Lake Erie into the Atlantic to show that the Great Lakes and the ocean were now linked.*

Buffalo into the waters of the Atlantic, as a symbol that the Great Lakes and the Atlantic Ocean had been joined.

Clinton, who was now at the peak of his career, was ready for higher office and was considered to have a chance at his party's nomination for the presidency of the United States. But Andrew Jackson had, in the meantime, become the most popular presidential candidate. It was soon recognized that Jackson would not be denied the nomination. In that case, Clinton could be his running mate or he could be appointed secretary of state, if Jackson were elected president. But before any of this could take place, De Witt Clinton died of a heart attack in February 1827. He was fifty-eight years old.

Even though the canal's great champion did not long survive its opening, "Clinton's Ditch" was now part of the American scene, and people were aware that a new era in the history of our country was beginning.

CHAPTER SIX

CANAL FEVER

THE JOURNEY OF THE SENECA CHIEF was the last sailing on the Erie Canal that year. Soon afterwards, the snow began to fly, forcing the canal to close. This was the pattern followed every year. Four feet of water can freeze into a solid mass very quickly. So at the first sign of ice or severe cold, boats took refuge in one of the many boat basins along the canal route and waited for the spring thaw to set them free to go about their business again.

And what a business it was. The small fleet of boats on the canal in 1825 grew to more than

BOATS WAITED IN SPECIAL BASINS *for warm weather in the spring to thaw out the frozen canal so that they could resume their business.*

3,000 by 1836 and 7,000 soon after the Civil War. And as the fleet grew, so did the money being collected by the state in tolls. By 1836, the entire construction cost of nearly $8 million had been repaid.

Each boat using the canal had to pay a toll according to the weight of its cargo and the distance traveled. Originally, there were three weighlocks along the canal's route, at Troy, Utica, and Syracuse, so no boat could escape paying the proper toll.

Boats entered a weighlock *building to determine the toll to be paid on their cargoes. This is the Oswego Weighlock in its last days.*

A boat to be weighed floated onto a giant scale inside an enclosed lock. When water was drained from the lock, the boat rested on a huge cradle suspended from a balance beam. The weight of the boat was registered accurately in the scale room next door. Then the weight of the empty boat, which was already known, was subtracted. The remainder was the weight of the cargo, and the toll was paid on that.

Growing traffic spread prosperity to the communities the canal served—and beyond. The Erie was now the main highway over which many thousands of merchants and traders traveled back and forth on business. It was the main funnel through which immigrants moved westward. This was the new blood the frontier needed to grow—Yankees leaving the rocky soil of New England for richer land, and people coming from foreign lands to settle or simply to see the marvelous canal.

"Canal boats filled with emigrants covered with goods and furniture arrive every day," a Buffalo newspaper reported. "Several steamboats depart daily for the far west crammed with masses of living beings to populate those regions. The eastern country was pouring out its millions for Ohio and Michigan." The Great Lakes were alive with steamboats moving people west where they would clear the forests, build their cabins, and plant their crops.

Eventually, our great inland cities of Cleveland, Chicago, Detroit, Toledo, and others would grow out of this mass movement. Even in Upper New York, cities such as Syracuse, Rochester, Buffalo, and Lockport sprouted where none existed before. They became great industrial centers. And the canal helped to make New York City the greatest port and the largest city in the United States.

Various tradesmen soon followed the new settlers into the remotest places. Besides the canal-side hotels and the grocery and boat supply stores that sprang up everywhere, there were floating shops of menders and tool makers and general stores that sold cloth, guns, needles, tools, clocks, and a thousand other things settlers needed. Even entertainers came to the frontier. Show companies traveled up and down the canal in boats with specially designed stages for giving performances.

Year after year, passengers and freight came sweeping inland, and western wheat, corn, furs, lumber, and cattle were shipped east. They were carried in several different types of craft. The most common were the "line" boats, which carried cargo from the west to the east, and on the return trip carried settlers with their livestock and belongings. Their cabins were tiny and cramped, too small for passengers to even turn around in. But the fare on

The Erie teemed with activity *and life. Shops, hotels, and other businesses that catered to the needs of workers and travelers sprouted along its route.*

A canal boat unloads *its cargo of grain at a storage elevator.*

one of these vessels was low, so they were favored by the poor and the frugal.

Those who could afford to pay more traveled on passenger "packet" boats. They were faster than other boats, and they were given first choice in going through the numerous locks. The packets could travel 80 miles (128 km) in twenty-four hours, double the distance of a line boat.

The greatest number of boats on the Erie were the freight carriers—scows to transport bulk cargo in an open hold and "bull heads" for such cargo as wheat and corn. The legal speed limit for freight boats was 2 1/2 miles (4 km) per hour.

There was one other type of boat on the Erie, the so-called "hurry up" boat, sent to make quick repairs anywhere a patrolling towpath walker noticed a leak or a break in the wall of the canal. A drop in the water level would bring traffic to a standstill. A "hurry up" boat would be rushed to the scene the moment a leak was detected to plug the hole before things got out of control.

In the peak years of its operation, the Erie employed more than 50,000 people. Half of these worked on the boats. The other half was made up of the locktenders, maintenance crews, and towpath walkers needed to keep the canal running smoothly, as well as the people who made their living from the shops that served the needs of travelers.

CANAL BOATS HAD NO ENGINES *or sails. They were pulled by a pair of sturdy mules or horses, usually driven by a boy who walked the towpath alongside the canal.*

A large number of young boys, called "hoggees," were employed to drive the mules and horses on the towpath. They worked two six-hour shifts every day, no matter what the weather. They took care of the animals and cooked their own meals. The pay for these boys was eight to ten dollars a month, given to them at the end of the season.

In just a few years, the Erie Canal was so heavily traveled it had become the nation's main street to the West. Cities, industries, and businesses sprouted along its path with amazing speed. And for the thousands of men, women, and children who traveled on its waters or worked on the boats and along the canal, the "canawlers," as they called themselves, the Erie was the most exciting place in the world, celebrated in stories and songs.

Success usually begets imitators. Seeing the prosperity the Erie was bringing to upper New York, people in other states caught "canal fever." Pennsylvania, Massachusetts, New Jersey, Virginia, Ohio, Delaware, and Michigan soon began building their own canals. Even New Yorkers demanded that a system of feeder canals be built to tie into the "Big Ditch." None of these was as successful as the Erie. The Erie continued to prosper, as thousands of horse-drawn boats sailed its calm waters, bringing great profit to New York state.

CHAPTER SEVEN

THE WAY TO GO

BOATS WITH SUCH CATCHY NAMES as *Noah's Ark, Young Lion of the West, Fair Play, Try and Catch Me*, and *Poor Richard* came down the Erie Canal one after the other, moving through the peaceful countryside that had until just recently been an unspoiled wilderness. For travelers, there was nothing like a ride in a canal boat. It was an unhurried way to go because the legal speed limit for packet boats was just 4 miles (6.4 km) an hour. Higher speeds were not permitted because waves would damage the sides of the canal. And the ride was completely safe. ☞

A PAINTING BY *Edward Lamson Henry shows passengers enjoying the countryside from the deck of a packet as it glides along the Erie.*

After all, what could happen to a boat in four feet of water?

The only noise passengers heard was the clopping of the horses' hoofs on the towpath and the gentle lapping of the water against the sides of the boat. Canal boats had no engines, so there was no clanging of wheels or hissing of steam to disturb the quiet. Boats were pulled by mules or horses, their number depending on the weight of the boat. Two or more animals, guided by a driver, walked on the towpath that ran parallel to the canal, pulling a towline attached to the boat. Fresh tow animals were provided every 12 to 15 miles (19 to 24 km) for packets and every 15 to 20 miles (24 to 32 km) for line boats.

There was an unpleasant side to canal travel. Boats were just 80 feet (24 m) long and 14 feet (4 m) wide. They were restricted to that size in order to fit into the locks. Space for passengers, therefore, was cramped, and comfort and privacy were at a minimum.

Passengers on the packets were accommodated in a box-shaped cabin lighted by windows along both sides. If they wanted to sightsee or to escape the confinement of the cabin, they could climb to the deck on top of the cabin.

The cabin was designed for maximum economy and flexibility. During the day, it was a dining room.

At night, mattresses were spread on the seats on either side of the huge center table, and a tier of bunks was suspended from the roof over the mattresses. Then there was another tier on top of that, sometimes as many as four. The writer Charles Dickens, who traveled the Erie in its heyday, thought the tiers of bunks were as "large" as book shelves.

Ladies slept in a separate area near the bow of the boat, screened from the men by a curtain. There was a kitchen and a bar in the back. The cabin could be home to forty to one hundred passengers, in addition to the captain, two drivers, two steersmen, and a cook for eight to twelve days.

No wonder people spent as much time as possible on the roof. It wasn't just a matter of comfort. The view of the forests that sometimes touched the banks of the canal or of the distant hills and the towns through which the boats glided noiselessly was a good reason to bring passengers on deck. But there was a catch: they had to take care to keep their heads.

The only real danger along the level stretches of the canal was the more than three hundred wooden bridges that spanned the waterway. They were built to help farmers whose fields had been split by the canal reach their properties or to cross country

THE ERIE INSPIRED MANY *popular songs and ballads. A favorite was "Low Bridge. Everybody Down," a warning often heard as boats approached a bridge.*

roads over the canal. To keep costs down, the bridges were built just 7 to 8 feet (2.5 m) above the water. People standing on deck were in danger of losing their heads or being "scraped" off the boat into the water. To prevent accidents, a crew member was stationed at the bow to act as lookout. Whenever he saw a bridge, he shouted a warning: "Low bridge ahead. Everybody down!"

CHAPTER EIGHT

THE CANAL ERA BEGINS TO FADE

IMMEDIATELY AFTER THE ERIE CANAL had gone to full operation, the canal commissioners realized that it was too small for the large number of boats using it. They suggested that the canal be enlarged and that double locks be built to permit two-way traffic, eliminating the constant boat jams in front of the locks.

Work on the enlargement was started in 1836. The channel was widened from 40 to 70 feet (12 to 21 m) and its depth increased from 4 to 7 feet (1.2 to 2.1 m). At the same time, all the locks were

The Erie was enlarged twice. *Top, digging the ditch, which would later be filled with water. Bottom, fixing the wall of a lock.*

made bigger than the original and two new weighlocks were added. These improvements permitted larger boats that carried heavier cargoes to use the waterway.

The enlargement was not completed until 1862, twenty-six years after it was started. That was because work had to be done while the canal was in full use, and this made construction slower and more difficult.

Even as business on the Erie was booming and the canal's promise to bring the sprawling young nation together was being fulfilled, a dark cloud appeared on the horizon. It was no bigger than a puff of black smoke, but in time it would bring major changes to our transportation system.

Steam locomotives pulling cars that ran on rails had begun to appear here and there in various parts of the country in the 1830s. But they were still going through a trial period and no one was quite sure what their future would be.

Gradually, the little locomotives used on these scattered railroad lines got better and more powerful, and they were now able to carry more passengers and freight. As with most new technology, they began to capture the imagination of the public.

What people liked best about the trains was the speed with which they moved over long distances.

Americans are by nature in a hurry to get from place to place, and the railroads were carrying passengers faster and doing it with greater comfort than the canal boats. A ten-day trip on the canal took only fifteen hours on the train. So it was natural that people began to consider canals old-fashioned. By the mid-1850s when a rail line connected New York City with Buffalo, the Erie's passenger business had vanished.

Even though passenger packets had disappeared from its waters, the Erie was still a booming freight carrier. Because canal boats could carry more cargo for less money than the railroads, they could easily compete when speed was not important. The Erie was so successful as a freight carrier, in fact, that in 1882 tolls were eliminated. Boats could now use it as a freeway.

Beginning in 1905, the Erie Canal was enlarged once again to serve as a barge canal. It was deepened to 14 feet (4 m), it was widened to 120 to 200 feet (36.5 to 61 m), and larger locks replaced the old. Much of its channel was straightened and relocated to use natural waterways, where possible.

There are many remains of the old Erie Canal. Some locks and sections of aqueducts survive. The aqueduct that crossed the Genesee River in

The Weighlock Building *in Syracuse is now home to the Erie Canal Museum.*

Rochester is now a bridge, and the Weighlock Building in Syracuse is the Erie Canal Museum. But towpaths have vanished, along with the packets and the line boats. Today's large, modern barges are either self-propelled or pushed by powerful tugboats.

Despite the changes that time has brought about, people have not stopped admiring the bold men who planned and built the Erie Canal over an unfriendly wilderness. The Erie was a great engineering achievement for its day, and it provided proof that American ingenuity was equal to any challenge.

But the Erie was more than a world-famous engineering marvel. Its builders set an example of leadership, inventiveness, and risk taking that has been admired and emulated by Americans ever since.

Above all, the Erie Canal is remembered for the role it played in pushing the West beyond the Appalachian Mountains all the way to the Mississippi River. Over this now vanished man-made river flowed a sweeping tide of humanity in search of a better life, and the commerce that helped the United States to bind together its far-reaching territories and to grow and prosper as a nation.

GLOSSARY

Aqueduct. A water-carrying bridge built to help the canal cross over a river or a low valley.

Barge. A flat-bottomed vessel used on canals or rivers to transport cargo.

Bow. The front part of a boat.

Bull head. A boat, easy to recognize because of its rounded bow, used exclusively to carry cargo.

Canal. A man-made waterway for boats.

Canawlers. The term people working on canal boats used to describe themselves; a mispronunciation of the word "canallers."

Civil engineer. A person who designs and constructs roads, bridges, canals, and other public works.

Cradle. Part of a scale in a weighlock used to weigh canal boats.

Embankment. A wall made of earth or stone raised on the side of a canal to hold water inside.

Feeder canal. A branch canal which leads into a main canal, such as the Erie.

Flotilla. A fleet of small boats.

Hatch. A small door on the gate of a lock which opens to empty the water inside.

Hoggee. A young boy in his early teens (or sometimes a man) who drove the animals used to tow the canal boats.

Hurry up boat. A fast emergency boat equipped to repair any break in the wall of the canal that might cause the water to flow out.

Lock. An enclosed space in a canal or river with gates at either end in which the level of the water can be changed to raise or lower a boat.

Line boat. A combination passenger and cargo boat that moved pioneers and their possessions westward and brought back products of the West on their return trip.

Locktender. A worker who operates the gates of a lock to raise or lower the level of water inside.

Packet boat. Carried passengers and mail regularly over a fixed route.

Rapids. The part of a river where the current flows very fast, usually over rocks.

Scow. A flat-bottomed boat with square ends that carried freight in an open hold.

Sluice gate. A small gate that allows water to flow slowly in or out of a lock or from a feeder stream into the canal. It is controlled by levers at the top of the gate.

Surveyor. A person who measures land to fix the path of a canal or road or the shape of an area and its boundaries.

Toll. A fee paid for the use of the canal, set according to the weight of the boat and the miles it is going to travel.

Towpath. A path along the bank of a canal or a river used by animals or people towing a boat.

Tugboat. A small, powerful boat used for pushing and towing barges and ships.

Weighlock. A giant scale inside a lock. When the water was drained out of the lock, the boat came to rest on a cradle, its weight was registered, and the proper toll (see entry) was paid.

For Further Reading

Andrist, Ralph. *The Erie Canal.* New York: American Heritage Publishing Co., 1964.

Hilts, Len. *Timmy O'Dowd and the Big Ditch.* New York: Harcourt Brace Jovanovich, 1988.

Phelan, Mary Kay. *Waterway West.* New York: Thomas Y. Crowell, 1977.

Spier, Peter. *The Erie Canal*. New York: Doubleday, 1970.

Stein, R. Conrad. *The Story of the Erie Canal.* Chicago: Childrens Press, 1985.

INDEX

About the Author

NICHOLAS NIRGIOTIS was born in Chicago where he has lived most of his life. He graduated from the University of Chicago. Nicholas Nirgiotis has been a teacher and freelance writer. Mr. Nirgiotis travels widely, most recently to East Africa. He is married and the father of two children.